Animals of the Rain Forest

RAIN FORESTS TODAY

Ted O'Hare

The rain forest is home to countless kinds of animals.

Rourke

Publishing LLC

Vero Beach, Florida 32964

www.rourkepublishing.com

PHOTO CREDITS: Pages 4, 16, 18, 19 (inset), 21 (both) ©James H. Carmichael; all other photos ©Lynn Stone

Editor: Frank Sloan

Cover and page design by Nicola Stratford

Library of Congress Cataloging-in-Publication Data

O'Hare, Ted, 1961-
  Animals of the rain forest / Ted O'Hare.
      p. cm. -- (Rain forests today)
  Includes bibliographical references (p.   ).
  ISBN 1-59515-152-4 (hardcover)
  1. Rain forest animals--Juvenile literature. I. Title. II. Series: O'Hare, Ted, 1961-
Rain forests today.
  QL112.O38 2004
  591.734--dc22

                                                    2004010761

Printed in the USA

CG/CG

Table of Contents

Animals at Home

Thousands of animals live in the world's tropical rain forests. Their homes are known as **habitats**. The climate in these habitats is wet, warm, and tropical.

The biggest tropical rain forests are in South America, West Africa, and Southeast Asia. The kinds of animals found in these forests depend on where the forests are.

A mother orangutan and her baby swing through the rain forest trees on the island of Borneo.

Tigers, orangutans, and clouded leopards live in Asian rain forests. Gorillas live only in African rain forests. South America's rain forest is home to jaguars and **macaws** and other parrots.

The green-winged macaw lives in the rain forest.

Gorillas live in the
rain forests of Africa.

Animals and Plants

All rain forest animals need plants in order to live. Plants provide shelter and food. Animals may eat plants. Or they may eat other animals that have eaten plants.

Animals spread plant seeds in their droppings. Insects and bats **pollinate** plants. This allows plants to make new plants.

A blood python of the Malay Peninsula swallows a plant-eating rodent.

9

Surviving in Rain Forests

Animals have ways of surviving in the rain forest. Some become **arboreal**. This means they live in trees. Iguanas, monkeys, parrots, and some snakes and frogs live in the treetops.

Many creatures can disguise themselves by **camouflage**. Their body colors blend with their surroundings. They may look like leaves, sticks, or bark.

No one is sure how many kinds of animals live in tropical rain forests. Some rain forests have never been explored!

The margay is a small, tree-loving cat of Latin America.

This anole's skin helps camouflage it against a rain forest branch.

Mammals

Many mammals live on the rain forest floor.
Anteaters and armadillos prowl on the ground.
Some animals live in the tops of the tallest trees.
Monkeys swing from tree to tree.

Bats, which are also mammals, live in rain forests.

Jaguars, tigers, clouded leopards, and ocelots
hunt **prey** in the rain forest, usually at night.

A jaguar overlooks its rain forest world from a tree limb.

A Sumatran tiger growls from
its jungle retreat.

Snakes and Lizards

Snakes and lizards live on the rain forest floor and in the trees above. They are **predators**. This means they eat other animals.

Snakes catch bats, birds, rodents, lizards, and other snakes. Lizards eat insects. Snake colors blend into the background. This makes them hard to see. They are well camouflaged.

Raindrops glisten on a green tree python of the New Guinea rain forest.

Frogs and Toads

Frogs and toads like the warmth, shade, and moisture of tropical rain forests.

The poison-arrow frog is dangerous to most animals that hunt. South American Indians use its poison on the tips of their arrows and darts.

The poison-arrow frog has bright colors. These colors warn other animals to stay away!

These poison-arrow frogs of Surinam are bright blue.

Birds

Most birds live at the top of the rain forest, in the **canopy**. In this world of branches, vines, and leaves, birds find and eat seeds, fruits, insects, and lizards. Many kinds of birds build nests in the canopy.

In clearings in the rain forest, people are able to see colorful parrots, toucans, and hummingbirds.

A toucan shows off its huge but lightweight bill.

A purple honey-creeper perches in a Trinidad rain forest.

Insects

The number of insects in tropical rain forests is huge. Some people believe there may be as many as 80 million different kinds.

Some of the most colorful insects are the thousands of tropical butterflies.

Walkingsticks make up another interesting group. These insects **mimic**, or look like, sticks!

Because there are many insects in the rain forest, there are also lots of bats. This is because insects are food for most bat species.

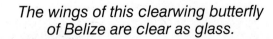

The wings of this clearwing butterfly of Belize are clear as glass.

Some insects mimic sticks, but this African ghost mantis looks like a dying leaf.

Animals in Danger

Tropical rain forests are being cut down to provide open land. This land is being used for farms, roads, and homes.

When the rain forest disappears, many kinds of animals are in danger. Their homes are disappearing, too. This means that many animals of the rain forest are in danger. Some animals may even become **extinct**.

Glossary

arboreal (ar BOR ee uhl) — referring to plants and animals that live in trees

camouflage (KAM uh flahj) — to blend in with one's surroundings

canopy (KAN uh pee) — the "roof" of upper branches of trees in a forest

extinct (EK stinkt) — no longer existing

habitats (HAB uh tatz) — special areas in which plants and animals live

macaws (muh KAWZ) — large parrots found mostly in Central and South America

mimic (MIM ik) — to imitate closely

pollinate (PAH lin ate) — the process by which certain insects, bats, and birds transfer pollen from one plant to another and help the plant to reproduce

predators (PRED uh turz) — animals that kill other animals for food

prey (PRAY) — an animal that is hunted to be food for another animal

Index

Further Reading

Frost, Helen. *Rain Forest Animals.* Six volumes. Capstone Press, 2002.
Patent, Dorothy Hinshaw. *Fabulous Fluttering Tropical Butterflies.* Walker, 2002.
Pringle, Laurence. *Bats! Strange and Wonderful.* Boyds Mills Press, 2000.

Websites to Visit

jajhs.kana.k12.wv.us/amazon/animal.htm
mbgnet.mobot.org/sets/rforest/animals/
www.enchantedlearning.com/subjects/rainforest/animals/Rfbiomeanimals.shtml
www.knowledgelink.com

About the Author

Ted O'Hare is an author and editor of children's nonfiction books. He divides his time between New York City and a home upstate.